This item is due for return on or before the last date below. It may be
renewed by telephone or in person if not required by another borrower.

Library   quality life yours

North
Lanarkshire
Council

Tree Frogs

By Erika and Jim Deiters

Raintree

www.raintreepublishers.co.uk
Visit our website to find out more information about Raintree books.

To order:
☎ Phone 44 (0) 1865 888112
🖹 Send a fax to 44 (0) 1865 314091
🖥 Visit the Raintree Bookshop at www.raintreepublishers.co.uk to browse our
catalogue and order online.

First published in Great Britain by
Raintree Publishers, Halley Court,
Jordan Hill, Oxford, OX2 8EJ, part of
Harcourt Education.
Raintree is a registered trademark of
Harcourt Education Ltd.

Originated by Dot Gradations
Printed and bound in China by South
China Printing

ISBN 1 844 21129 0
07 06 05 04 03
10 9 8 7 6 5 4 3 2 1

British Library Cataloguing in Publication Data
Deiters, Erika & Jim
1. Hylidae – Juvenile literature
2. Rainforest ecology – Juvenile
literature
597.8'78
A catalogue for this book is available
from the British Library.

Acknowledgements
The publishers would like to thank the
following for permission to reproduce
photographs:
Digital Stock Photos, p. **1**. Hemera/
Photobjects p. **7**. Root Resources/
Anthony Merceica, p. **8**; A.B. Sheldon.
Unicorn Stock Photos/Ron Holt, p. **12**.
Visuals Unlimited/Joe McDonald, pp. **19**,
28; William J. Weber p. **11**; William
Palmer, p. **15**; John Serrao; James
Beveridge, p. **22**; Nathan W. Cohen,
p. **24**; Erwin C. 'Bud' Nielsen, p. **26**

Cover photograph reproduced with
permission of Corbis/Darren Maybury;
Eye Ubiquitous

Every effort has been made to contact
copyright holders of any material
reproduced in this book. Any omissions
will be rectified in subsequent printings
if notice is given to the publishers.

Contents

Any words appearing in the text in bold, **like this**, are explained in the Glossary.

large eyes
see pages 7, 15

long toes
see pages 7, 14

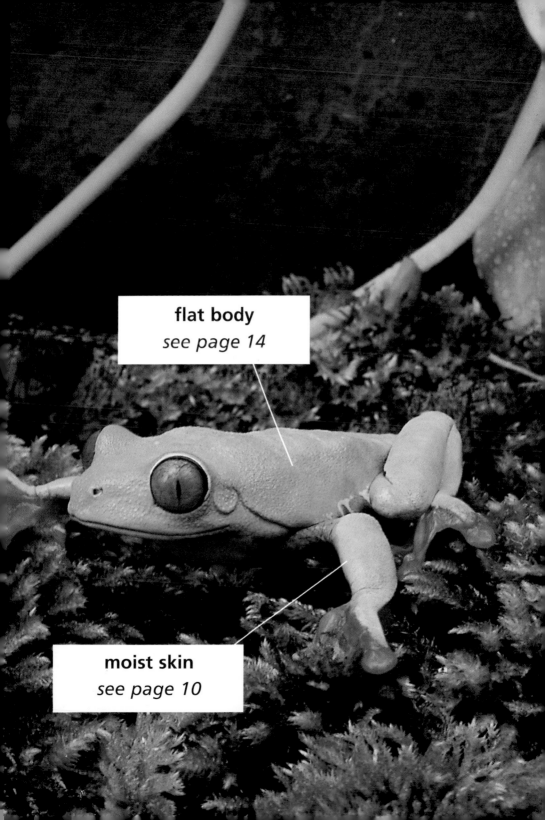

flat body
see page 14

moist skin
see page 10

North Atlantic
Ocean

USA

MEXICO

BELIZE
GUATEMALA   HONDURAS
EL SALVADOR   Caribbean Sea
              NICARAGUA

COSTA RICA
PANAMA

VENEZUELA
              SURINAM
COLOMBIA   GUYANA   FRENCH GUIANA

ECUADOR
              Amazon River

PERU

BRAZIL

BOLIVIA

PARAGUAY

South Pacific
Ocean

URUGUAY

CHILE   ARGENTINA

South Atlantic
Ocean

Range of the
green tree frog

Range of the
glass tree frog

Surrounding land

Sea

Borders

Rivers

6

A quick look at tree frogs

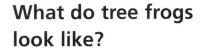

What do tree frogs look like?

Tree frogs have long fingers and toes. They have large eyes. They can be many different colours.

Where do tree frogs live?

Tree frogs live all over the world. More tree frogs live in the rainforests of Central and South America than anywhere else.

What do tree frogs eat?

Tree frogs eat almost any animal they can fit in their mouths. They eat spiders, flies, moths and worms.

How many kinds of tree frogs are there?

There are more than 500 kinds of tree frogs. They are many different sizes. Scientists are still finding new kinds of tree frogs.

The sticky pads on this tree frog's toes
help it hold on to this leaf.

Tree frogs in rainforests

Tree frogs are **amphibians**. Amphibians are animals that live both in the water and on the land. Most amphibians begin their lives in the water. They move to land as adults. Adult tree frogs move from the land into the trees. They have sticky pads on their toes that help them to climb.

Tree frogs and all amphibians are **cold-blooded**. The body temperature of cold-blooded animals is about the same as the air or water around them. Temperature is a measure of hot and cold.

Tree frogs need the heat to warm their bodies. They need to warm their bodies to make their muscles work.

About tree frogs

Water is important in the lives of tree frogs. They need to lay their eggs in water. Water keeps their skin moist. The skin on a tree frog's back, legs and stomach soaks up water into its body.

There are more than 500 **species** of tree frog. They are all sorts of different sizes and colours. Many are brightly coloured. Scientists are still finding new species of tree frogs.

Tree frogs are important in nature. They help control the number of insects. Snakes, birds and bats eat tree frogs. Some snakes eat tree frog eggs.

Where tree frogs live

Tree frogs live all over the world. They need to live in warm wet places. There are no tree frogs in Antarctica. It is too cold and dry there.

Warm rainforests are perfect homes for tree frogs. The rainforests of Central and South

Water soaks into frogs' bodies through their skin to keep them moist.

America are home to the most kinds of tree frogs. Rainforests are places where lots of trees and plants grow close together and rain falls nearly every day. Many different kinds of animals live in rainforests.

▲ This tree frog is sitting in a tree among leaves. Its colouring makes it hard to see.

Life in trees

Most tree frogs live in trees. They find food in trees. They climb trees to escape from **predators**. Predators hunt and eat other animals. The animals that predators eat are called prey.

Not all tree frogs live in trees. Some tree frogs make their homes in tall grasses and short bushes. Other tree frogs do not climb at all. The cricket tree frog of North America spends most of its time on the ground in wet areas.

What tree frogs look like

The most common colour for tree frogs is green to blend in with leaves. They also can be blue, red, yellow, orange and other colours. Some tree frogs have markings. A marking is a pattern on an animal. Most tree frogs can change their colour to match their backgrounds. This is called **camouflage**. Camouflage helps the tree frogs hide from predators.

Tree frogs can be many sizes. Some tree frogs are less than 2.5 centimetres long. Others are as long as 14 centimetres. Female tree frogs may be twice the size of males.

Special body parts

Tree frogs have long toes made for climbing. Sticky pads on the ends of their toes help them grip leaves and branches. The White's tree frog of Australia is a great climber. It can even climb glass.

Most tree frogs are longer and thinner than other frogs. Their bodies are also flatter. Their shape helps tree frogs balance. Balance is the ability to be steady and not fall. Good balance allows tree frogs to move easily through trees.

Some types of tree frog

The glass frog is an unusual kind of tree frog. It lives in the rainforests of Costa Rica. The skin of this tree frog is transparent. Transparent means you can see through it. The heart and lungs of the glass frog are visible through its skin.

The rainforests of Central America are home to the red-eyed tree frog. These frogs are known for their large red eyes. Yellow-eyed tree frogs also live in these rainforests. They are known for their large yellow eyes.

▲ **This is a glass frog from the rainforests of Costa Rica.**

Some tree frogs are nicknamed flying tree frogs. But these frogs do not really fly. They leap into the air and glide. They use their webbed toes to steer. Their sticky toe pads help them land.

This tree frog is eating a moth. Tree frogs eat mainly insects.

Food

Tree frogs will eat any animal that fits in their mouths. They eat ants, caterpillars, spiders, moths, flies, snails and worms. Tree frogs may also eat fruits and plants.

Tree frogs must be careful about what animals they eat. Many ants in the rainforest can sting. Some rainforest caterpillars are poisonous. Tree frogs can become ill or die if they eat anything poisonous.

Some tree frogs are fussy eaters. Smaller tree frogs may eat only ants or termites. One kind of tree frog in the rainforest of Brazil eats only berries.

Hunting and eating

Tree frogs look for food at night. They sleep during the day. Tree frogs are hungry when they wake up. They can eat a hundred insects in a night.

Tree frogs are good hunters. They climb quietly through branches looking for prey. Tree frogs can see and hear well. Scientists think tree frogs may be able to smell prey. Tree frogs can also feel nearby prey. The smallest movement tells tree frogs where prey is.

Tree frogs move in close once they find prey. They shoot out their sticky tongues to grab prey. Their tongues can be as long as their heads. Their tongues are attached to the front of their mouths. Tree frogs have small teeth in their mouths to hold prey.

Tree frogs do not chew their prey. Instead, tree frogs swallow their prey whole. Stomach juices then break down whatever the tree frogs have swallowed.

Tree frogs climb plant stems and trees to look for prey.

Tree frogs' throats fill with air when they call to mates.

A tree frog's life cycle

Tree frogs mate at the beginning of the **rainy season**. The rainy season is a time of year when it rains almost every day in the rainforest. Tree frogs need the rain so they can lay their eggs. Males find pools of water and then attract females.

Male tree frogs use special calls to attract females. Large groups of calling males are known as a chorus. Each kind of tree frog has a special call. Tree frogs can tell the difference between these calls.

A red-eyed tree frog laid these eggs on a leaf. Tadpoles are growing inside them.

Eggs

The female tries to hide the eggs she lays. Some tree frogs lay twenty or thirty eggs, and some lay thousands. Females may hide the eggs in the water. They may place them near grass, behind water plants or next to rocks.

Most eggs hatch after six to eight days. Only a few of the eggs will develop into adult frogs. Most of the eggs are eaten by fish.

Some tree frogs do not need to be in the water to lay eggs. Female red-eyed tree frogs lay their eggs on the underneath of leaves that hang over water. Other kinds of tree frogs lay eggs in water trapped in branches or leaves.

Young

Young tree frogs are called **tadpoles**. Tadpoles look like small fish. They get oxygen through gills. Oxygen is a gas that all animals need in order to live. Gills are body parts that take oxygen from water. Tadpoles and fish get oxygen the same way.

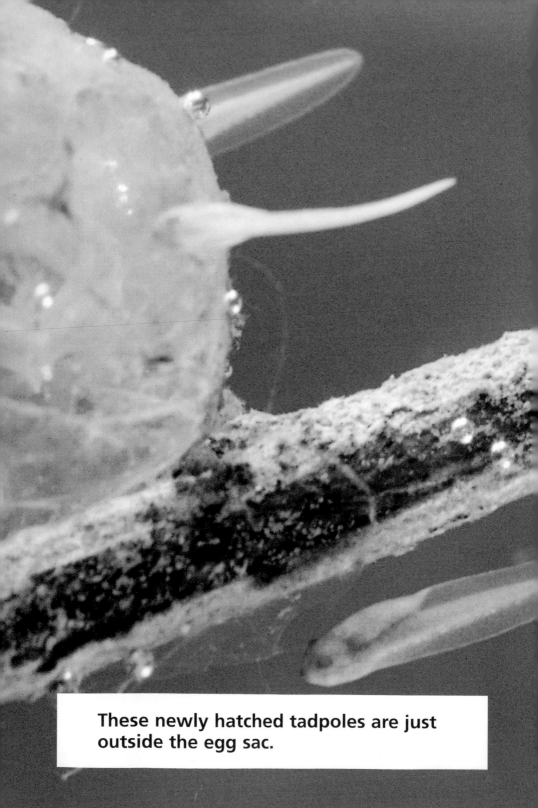

These newly hatched tadpoles are just outside the egg sac.

Tadpoles

Tadpoles live in water for up to fourteen weeks. At first they eat their remaining egg gel. They then eat mostly algae. Algae are small rootless plants that grow in water or on damp surfaces.

Tadpoles must look out for predators. Water birds, fish and snakes eat tadpoles.

Tadpoles breathe underwater using their gills. Gills are part of the tadpole's body that can absorb oxygen directly from water.

Tadpoles change in the water. They begin to grow legs. They grow lungs. They also begin to lose their tails.

Tadpoles leave the water as **froglets**. A froglet is a young tree frog with a short tail. The froglet's tail gets absorbed into its body. The tail becomes food for the growing tree frog. The froglet's gills disappear. After a short time, the froglet becomes an adult tree frog.

The length of time a tree frog lives depends on what kind it is. Some tree frogs kept as pets can live for 25 years.

This pet tree frog is holding on to its owner's finger.

Living with tree frogs

Tree frogs help people. They eat insects. People also use tree frogs to forecast the weather. Male tree frogs call for females at the start of the rainy season. People of the rainforest listen for the mating calls. Then they know that rain is coming.

Some people keep tree frogs as pets. Most owners keep tree frogs in glass aquariums filled with leaves and branches. Owners feed tree frogs crickets and mealworms. Mealworms are the **larvae** of some kinds of beetles. A larva is the young stage of an insect. It looks like a worm.

▲ Tree frogs cannot live in the rainforest if their habitats are taken away.

Medicine

Scientists have found a medicine in the skin of the White's tree frog. The medicine cures cold sores. A cold sore is a kind of sore on a person's face near or in the mouth.

Dying out

Many tree frogs are dying out. People are cutting down their **habitats**. A habitat is the surroundings that an animal or plant needs to survive. People are clearing rainforest trees to make room for roads and farms. They are also selling the wood. Tree frogs need the safety of leaves and branches. Some kinds of tree frogs may die out before we even know about them.

Tree frogs' bodies can be changed by pollution. Pollution is harmful material made by people. It is found in air, water or soil. Pollution thins the air and makes the sun too hot for tree frogs. Tree frogs' bodies take in poisons from the water. Scientists have found tree frogs with extra legs and missing eyes.

Knowing what harms tree frogs may help people to understand pollution in nature. Pollution that changes frogs could affect people in the future. Helping the tree frogs live will also help people.

Glossary

amphibian (am-FIB-ee-uhn) animal that begins life in the water and later lives on the land

camouflage colours, shapes and patterns that help an animal or plant blend in with the things around it

cold-blooded animal with a body temperature that changes according to its surroundings

froglet stage in a frog's growth when it first moves on to land

habitat surroundings that an animal or plant needs to survive

larva young stage of an insect, which looks like a worm

predator animal that hunts other animals to eat

rainy season period of time when it rains almost every day in the rainforest; forests and grasslands flood during the rainy season

species group of animals or plants most closely related to each other

tadpole stage in a frog's growth when it is living in the water

More information

Internet sites

Animals of the Rainforest
www.animalsoftherainforest.org

Rainforest Concern
www.rainforestconcern.org

Useful address

Rainforest Concern
27 Lansdowne Crescent
London
W11 2NS

Books to read
Interfact Geography: Rainforests (Book/CDROM)
    Heinemann Library, Oxford, 2001

Theodorou, R; Telford, C. *Amazing Journeys:
Up a Rainforest Tree*. Heinemann Library,
Oxford, 1998

Index